CREATE YOUR OWN

AFFIRMATIONS

A Creative Visualization Kit

SHAKTI GAWAIN

Nataraj Publishing
a division of

NEW WORLD LIBRARY
NOVATO, CALIFORNIA

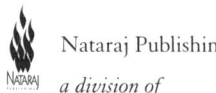

Nataraj Publishing
a division of

New World Library
14 Pamaron Way
Novato, California 94949

Package design by Mary Ann Casler
Text design and typography by Tona Pearce Myers
Edited by Vanessa Brown

First Printing September 2003
Package ISBN 1-57731-434-4
Printed in Thailand
Distributed by Publishers Group West

10 9 8 7 6 5 4 3 2 1

CONTENTS

THE BASIC TECHNIQUE OF
CREATIVE VISUALIZATION

—•◆•—

Creative visualization is the art of using imagination and affirmation to produce positive changes in your life. The fundamental process of creative visualization is simply to imagine as clearly and realistically as possible what you want to happen, as if it has already happened or is already happening, thus creating an inner experience of what it would be like to have your desire come true. This process is really so simple that you can do it at any moment, just by closing your eyes (or by leaving them open, if you prefer) and imagining your desired goal as if it were already true. No fancy techniques at all are required in order to do this, and ultimately you can incorporate creative visualization as part of your natural way of thinking and living moment by moment.

Here is the most basic creative visualization technique, in four steps:

Step 1. Pick a goal, something that you desire to be, do, or have. For example: "I would like to be more assertive."

Step 2. Make an affirmation out of it. State it in a simple sentence, in the present tense, as if it were already true. For example: "I am an assertive person."

Step 3. Imagine your goal or feel it as if it were already true. Usually it's helpful to close your eyes and just pretend or imagine what things would be like if it were true. Don't worry if you can't picture the scenario clearly, just feel it or imagine it in whatever way is easiest for you. *It is not necessary to see mental pictures in order to use creative visualization successfully.* Many people just think about, or sense, their desired goal rather than seeing a mental picture.

Step 4. Consciously turn your goal over to your higher self, or to the higher power of the universe, and let go of it. This means you don't try to *make* it happen; you relax and *let* the higher force go to work within you to create it. Then just go about your life — but be sure to follow your intuitive impulses and prompting, and be open to growing and changing.

How to Enjoy Creating Goals

———•◆•———

Every time you have a desire, in a certain sense you have a goal — something that you would like to be, do, or have. Some desires are merely passing fancies, but others stay with us and go deeper. Our desires and goals give us a direction and focus; they help to point us down our path of action in life.

For many people, the word "goal" has a negative connotation because it has so often been associated with compulsiveness, pushing, driving ourselves, competing with others, and so on. And truly, goals are often very much misused. But you can't really avoid having goals anyway (even if your goal is just to have no goals, or just to be in the moment, or to meditate all day, that's still a goal!). So you might as well learn to use and enjoy them.

To enjoy your goals, think of them as signposts pointing you in a certain direction. They give you a certain focus and help your energy to get moving. The *way* you get there is up to you. You could get very uptight along the way, focusing only on arriving at your goal, *or* you could relax and enjoy the journey itself, appreciating each step of the way, every unexpected bend and turn of the road, and every new opportunity for learning something.

So go ahead and play with setting goals, when and if you want to. See how this feels to you and whether it helps you or not. If you are already a very organized, goal-oriented person and you tend to use goals to control your life and stifle your spontaneity, it might be better to make your only goal be to relax and act spontaneously for a while. But if you tend to be disorganized, or have a hard time getting into action, setting goals may really help you. It's a very individual thing.

Guidelines for Setting Goals

- With short-range goals, be realistic. Don't set them too high, or you'll end up feeling discouraged. It's best to take a short, reachable step first, to create a feeling of confidence.

- With long-range goals, be expansive and idealistic. Let your imagination open up and reach for the highest. This will inspire you.

- Put your main focus on the *essence* of the goal. Don't worry about the details, as those may change.

- Don't be compulsive about your goals. In other words, don't try to *make* them happen. Hold them lightly, relax, and *let* them happen at their own pace and in their own way. Turn them over to your higher self to create them, and *let go.*

- Be flexible. You will probably find that many of your goals change frequently, but that there is an essence in the most important ones that remains the same, and which helps guide you ever closer to your highest purposes.

The Goals Process

This goals process is useful to practice at least once. You may want to repeat it every six months or once a year, perhaps, just to see how things change for you over time. Its purpose is to open up and expand your imagination, as well as to help you focus on what things are truly most important to you.

Think about your goals for the next month, six months, year, two years, five years, ten years, and for your life. Write each goal in the form of an affirmation — that is, write it in a sentence, in the *present* tense, as if it has already come true. This will make it a powerful process of creative visualization. So instead of saying, "I *want to* live in a bigger, sunnier, more beautiful apartment," you would phrase it this way, "I *am now* living in a big, beautiful, sunny apartment that I love."

When you write your short-range goals (one month, two months, six months), try to be realistic; choose goals that you can *fairly* easily accomplish. If you set your standards too high, you may feel discouraged in a month or two if everything doesn't happen. With longer-range goals (especially five years, ten years, lifetime), allow yourself to be as expansive as feels right to you.

When I first did this process, I thought it would be impossible to know what my long-range goals would be. ("How am I going to know what I'll want in five or ten years?") But I started doing it, and I was amazed at how much came out of it for me. So just think of this as a playful learning experience.

Prioritizing Goals

This is a process you can do on a regular basis, say once a month, or any time you just want to take a look at what's most important to you at the time, and where your highest priorities are. Simply list the five or six most important goals in your life at the current time, that is, things that you would like to put your energy into right now or in the near future. Some of these may be short-term goals, some may be long-term, but they are the ones you feel most strongly about at the moment.

USING AFFIRMATIONS TO
MANIFEST YOUR GOALS

•••

Affirmations are one of the most important elements of creative visualization. To affirm means "to make firm." An affirmation is a strong, positive statement that something is already so. It is a way of "making firm" that which you are imagining.

Most of us are aware of the fact that we have a nearly continuous inner dialogue going on in our minds. The mind is busy talking to itself, keeping up an endless commentary about life, the world, our feelings, our problems, and other people. The words and ideas that run through our minds are very important. Most of the time we aren't consciously aware of this stream of thoughts, and yet what we are telling ourselves in our minds is the basis on which we form our experience of reality. Our mental commentary influences and colors our feelings and perceptions about what's going on in our lives, and it is these thought forms that ultimately attract and create everything that happens to us.

Anyone who has practiced meditation knows how difficult it can be to quiet this inner chatter in order to connect with our deeper, wiser intuitive mind. One traditional meditation practice involves simply observing the inner dialogue as objectively as possible. This is a very valuable experience, as it allows you to become consciously aware of the content of your thoughts. Many of these thoughts are like recordings of old patterns we've had all our lives. They are old programming we picked up long ago, which is still influencing what's happening to us today. For example, we might find that we habitually think self-defeating thoughts such as, "I'm not going to be able to do this," or, "This is never going to work out right." The practice of engaging in affirmations allows us to begin replacing some of our stale, worn out, or negative mind chatter with more positive ideas and concepts. It is a powerful technique, one which can in a short time transform many of our attitudes and expectations about life, and thereby help to change what we create for ourselves.

Affirmations can be done silently, spoken aloud, written down, or even sung or chanted. Even ten minutes a day of repeating effective affirmations can counterbalance years of old mental habits. If you become aware that you are repeating habitual negative thought patterns or attitudes, try saying an affirmation to yourself a few times right then and there. For example, if you find yourself thinking, "Oh, what's the use, I'll never get what I want," you might say to yourself, "I have the ability to create what I want in my life" or, "I deserve to be happy and fulfilled." An affirmation can be any positive statement. It can be very general or very specific. There are an infinite number of possible affirmations; find the ones that work for you.

Guidelines for Using Affirmations

- Always phrase affirmations in the present tense, not in the future. It's important to create your desire as if it already exists. Don't say, "I will get a wonderful new job," but rather, "I now have a wonderful new job." This is not lying to yourself; it is acknowledging the fact that everything is created first on the inner plane, before it can manifest in external reality.

- Always phrase affirmations in the most positive way you can. Affirm what you do want, not what you don't want. Don't say, "I no longer oversleep in the morning," but rather, "I now wake up on time and full of energy in the morning." This ensures that you are creating the most positive possible mental image. At certain times you may find it helpful to phrase affirmations negatively, especially when you are working on clearing out specific emotional blocks or bad habits, such as, "I don't need to get tense in order to get things accomplished." If so, you should always follow this type of affirmation with a positive one, which describes that which you desire to create, such as, "I now stay deeply relaxed and centered, and everything is accomplished easily and effortlessly."

- In general, the shorter and simpler the affirmation, the more effective. An affirmation should be a clear statement that conveys a strong feeling; the more feeling it conveys, the stronger impression it makes on your mind. Affirmations that are long, wordy, and theoretical lose their emotional impact and become too mental.

- Always choose affirmations that feel totally right for you. What works for one person may not work at all for another. An affirmation should feel positive, expansive, freeing, and/or supportive. If it doesn't, find another one, or try changing the words until it feels right. Of course, you may feel emotional resistance to any affirmation when you first use it, especially one that is really powerful for you and is going to make a real change in your consciousness. That is simply our natural fear of change and growth.

- Always remember that you are creating something new and fresh. You are not trying to redo or change what already exists. To do so would be to resist what is, which creates conflict and struggle. Take the attitude that you are accepting and handling whatever already exists in your life, and at the same time taking every moment as a new opportunity to begin creating exactly what you desire and will make you happiest.

- Affirmations are not meant to contradict or change your feelings or emotions. It is important to accept and experience all your feelings, including so-called negative ones, without attempting to change them. At the same time, affirmations can help you create a new point of view about life that will enable you to have more and more satisfying experiences from now on.

- Try as much as possible to create a feeling of belief, an experience that your affirmations can be true. Temporarily (at least for a few minutes) suspend your doubts and hesitations, and put your full mental and emotional energy into your affirmations. If doubts, resistance, or negative thoughts are getting in the way, do a clearing process. Rather than saying affirmations by rote, try to get the feeling that you really have the power to create that reality (which in fact you do!). This will make a big difference in how effective they are.

Affirmations can be used alone, or in combination with visualizing or imaging. It's very effective to include affirmations as part of your regular creative visualization meditation periods.

For many people, affirmations are most powerful and inspiring when they include references to a spiritual source. Mention of God, the Goddess, the Universe, a higher power, spirit, the Earth Mother, divine love, or whatever phrase you prefer adds spiritual energy to your affirmation and acknowledges the universal source of all things. Here are some examples:

*I have the infinite creative power
of the Goddess within me.*

*Divine love is working through me here and now
to create this.*

*The Christ within me is creating miracles
in my life here and now.*

I am one with the Great Spirit.

My higher self is guiding me in everything that I do.

*God lives within me and manifests
in the world through me.*

*I give thanks to Mother Earth
for nurturing and sustaining me every day.*

*The light of God surrounds me, the love of God
enfolds me, the power of God flows through me.
Wherever I am, God is, and all is well!*

Ways to Use Affirmations

There are so many ways that affirmations can be used powerfully and effectively to give you a more positive, creative outlook and to help you achieve specific goals. Remember, it's important to feel relaxed as you affirm. Do not be addicted to getting the results you expect.

Meditation

Say affirmations to yourself silently while meditating or relaxing deeply, especially right before going to sleep or right after waking up.

Spoken

1. Say them to yourself silently or aloud throughout the day, whenever you think of it, especially while driving, doing housework, or during other routine tasks.

2. Say them to yourself aloud while looking at yourself in the mirror. This is especially good for affirmations to improve your self-esteem and self-love. Look yourself right in the eyes and affirm your beauty, lovableness, and worthiness. If you feel uncomfortable, stick with it until you push through those barriers

and are able to fully experience looking at yourself and loving yourself. You may find that some emotion arises and is released through this process.

3. Record your affirmations and play them to yourself around the house, while driving, and so on. Use your name, and try doing them in the first, second, and third persons. Or you can record a little speech, maybe three or four paragraphs long, describing your ideal visualization of yourself or a particular situation, as if it were already true. This also can be done in the first, second, and/or third person.

With Others

1. If you have a friend who wants to work on affirmations as well, you can do them very effectively with a partner. Sit facing each other, look into each other's eyes, and take turns saying affirmations to each other and accepting them.

Tom: "Anita, you are a beautiful, loving, and creative person."

Anita: "Yes, I know!" or "Yes, I am!"

Repeat this ten or fifteen times the same way, then switch partners so that Anita says the affirmation to Tom and he agrees with it. Then try it in the first person.

Tom: "I, Tom, am a beautiful, loving, and creative person."

Anita: "Yes, you certainly are."

Repeat several times. Be sure to say the affirmations sincerely and meaningfully, even if you feel a little silly at first. It's a wonderful opportunity to outflow love and support to another person, and to really support the other person in changing his or her negative concepts into positive ones. It's practically guaranteed that after doing this process together, you will be experiencing a deep, loving space together.

2. In a more informal way, ask your friends to say affirmations to you frequently. For example, if you want to affirm that you are learning to express yourself more easily, you might ask a good friend to say to you often, "Jennifer, you are certainly speaking out and expressing yourself clearly these days!"

3. Make a game out of doing this for each other and you will find it helpful. We automatically tend to give a lot of power to what our

friends say to us, for good or bad; our minds tend to accept what others tell us about ourselves. So getting strong positive feedback from friends in the form of affirmations really works.

4. Begin to include affirmations in your conversations. Make strong, positive statements about things and people (including yourself) that you want to see in a more positive way. It's amazing what dramatic changes can be made in your life by just beginning to consciously speak more positively in daily conversation.

5. A word of caution: do not use this technique in such a way that you feel like you are contradicting your true feelings. Do not use it when you are feeling upset or strongly negative or it will feel like you are repressing yourself. Employ it from a constructive space, to help change your unconscious negative speech patterns and underlying assumptions.

Singing & Chanting

Make a point of learning songs or chants that affirm the reality you would like to create for yourself; listen to them and sing them often. Seek out positive messages, or make up your own songs or simple chants using the affirmations you want to work with.

Written

Take any affirmation you want to work with and write it ten or twenty times in succession on a journal page. Use your name, and also try writing it in the first, second, and third persons. Remember to use the present tense. For example:

I, Jane, have now finished my first watercolor painting.
Jane, you have now finished your first watercolor painting.
Jane has now finished her first watercolor painting.

Don't just write it by rote; really think about the meaning of the words as you write them. Notice whether you feel any resistance, doubts, or negative thoughts about what you are writing. Whenever you do (even slightly), turn the page, and on the back write out the negative thought, the reason why the affirmation can't be true, can't work, or whatever. For example: *I'm really not good enough,* or *I'm too old,* or *This isn't going to work.*

Then go back to writing the affirmation. When you are finished, take a look at the back of the page. If you have been honest, you will have a good look at the reasons why you are keeping yourself from having what you want in this particular case. With this in mind, make up some affirmations you can use to help you counteract, or clear, these negative fears or beliefs, and begin to write out these new affirmations. Or you may want to stick with your original affirmation if it seems effective, or modify it slightly to be more accurate.

Keep working with writing the affirmations once or twice a day for a few days. Once you feel that you've really looked at your negative beliefs, discontinue writing out negative thoughts, and keep writing just the affirmations.

Create Your Own Affirmation Cards

Using the guidance above, compose an affirmation in your journal. Refine the statement until it sounds right to you, and feel free to continue to modify the affirmation as you go along if you think of better ways to say it. The writing process will help you create affirmations that are most effective for your specific goals.

When you find an affirmation that works particularly well for you, use one of the enclosed cards to create your own affirmation reminder. You can build your own deck of favorite affirmations, and display them in various places around your home or at your work, to help you visualize your goals. Good places to post your cards are on the refrigerator, on a phone, on your mirror, on your desk, over your bed, or on the dining table — anywhere you will see them in the course of your routine. You can also keep a special affirmation with you by tucking the card into your backpack, wallet, organizer, pillowcase, lunch bag, or coat pocket — anyplace you will encounter it.

CLEARING THE PATH TO SUCCESSFUL CREATIVE VISUALIZATION

•●•

The creative power of the universe is always trying to move through us, to create through us. The clearer and more aligned with our higher selves we are, the more easily that creative energy can move through to help us manifest our hearts' desires. But that creative power has to filter through our beliefs, attitudes, emotions, and habits. The more negative and constricted our beliefs and patterns are, the more they block, slow, and distort the creative energy.

Clearing

One of the most important aspects of using creative visualization is the clearing process — letting go of false, constricting beliefs and replacing them with positive, supportive ones.

Clearing has to take place ultimately on all levels: physical, emotional, mental, and spiritual. There are many methods of clearing, including many forms of psychotherapy, bodywork and massage, yoga, various forms of exercise and breathing, psychic energy work and healing, and so on. I have used many of these methods myself and have found some of them to be powerful and important in my process. I recommend that you follow your own intuitive feelings about what kinds of clearing processes you may need at any given time.

The underlying principle in most forms of clearing is that you must recognize and be willing to fully acknowledge and experience any repressed negativity in your body, emotions, mind, and spirit, in order to fully release it. Most people hope that by ignoring negativity, it will go away, but the reverse is actually true! The harder you try to ignore it, the more it tends to come up in your life. It's as if all the dark places inside of you are actually trying to pull the light of consciousness to them, so they then can get cleaned out. The cleaning-out or clearing process happens through simply shining that light of awareness into the dark places and being willing to experience what is there. Through experiencing it, the blocked energy is released.

So the more willing you are to face, own, and consciously experience your negative beliefs and patterns without judging yourself for them, the more quickly they will get cleared out.

The following are some simple clearing processes that you can do by yourself.

The Basic Clearing Process

This is the most basic clearing process, which you can use any time you have a goal or desire that you feel may be blocked.

First, state your goal in the form of an affirmation.

Second, write, "The reasons I can't have what I want are:" and then start listing every thought that comes into your head, no matter how silly, weird, terrible, or insignificant it seems. List as many reasons as you possibly can.

Third, once you have written out all the reasons you can possibly think of (and you may want to leave it and come back several times with more thoughts), sit for a while and look at your list. Decide which of the negative statements have the most power over you, and make a mark by those.

Then write an affirmation to counteract each one. Focus on the affirmations that feel most powerful to you, and meditate on them every day for a while, along with your original goal/affirmation.

Practice the basic clearing process with a goal of your own. Pick one that you have some resistance, fears, or doubts about being able to create.

Forgiving & Releasing Others

Write down the names of everyone in your life whom you feel has ever mistreated you, harmed you, done you an injustice, or toward whom you feel or have felt resentment, hurt, or anger. Next to each person's name, write down what they did to you, or what you resent them for. Then close your eyes, relax, and one-by-one visualize or imagine each person. Hold a little conversation with each one, and express the anger and hurt that you have felt. Tell them exactly what they have done to upset you, and what you want from them. Once you have done this, explain to them that now you are going to do your best to forgive them for everything, and to dissolve and release all constricted energy between you. Give them a blessing and say, *I forgive you and release you. Go your own way and be happy.* When you have finished this process, write across the paper, *I now forgive you and release you all.*

Forgiving & Releasing Yourself

Write down everyone you can think of in your life whom you feel you have hurt or done an injustice to, and write down what you did to them. Again, close your eyes, relax, and imagine each person in turn. Tell him or her what you did, and ask them to forgive you and give you their blessing. Then picture them doing so. When you have finished the process, write at the bottom of your paper (or across the whole thing), *I forgive myself and absolve myself of all guilt.*

Core Negative Beliefs

When people learn that they create their own reality, and that by focusing their minds on positive images and thoughts they can create a more positive reality, they sometimes become afraid of their negative thoughts. They fear that if they have a negative thought or idea, they are going to create that in their lives. Often people try to suppress or ignore their negative thoughts, and valiantly try to focus only on the positive. I believe that this is a mistake. Our negative thoughts are valuable messages to us about our deeper fears and negative attitudes. Negative thoughts that you are *consciously aware of* do not cause real problems. Once you are conscious of them, they are already on their way to being cleared out. It's the negative beliefs that we hold at deeper levels *without* conscious awareness that cause negative experiences in our lives and prevent us from creating what we consciously want.

The real troublemakers are our core negative beliefs — the deepest and most fundamental assumptions and expectations we have about life, the world, others, and ourselves. These core negative beliefs are usually so basic to our thinking and feeling that we don't even realize they are beliefs at all; we assume that they are simply the true nature of reality, just the way life is. As long as we have these unrecognized, deep-seated beliefs, they continue to govern the way we create our reality. So for example, you may be consciously affirming and visualizing prosperity, but if your unconscious belief is that you don't deserve it, or that it's immoral or unspiritual, then you won't create it.

So your negative thoughts and worries can be used positively if you are willing to be conscious of them and look deeper, to see what lies underneath them. Once you become *aware* of your core negative beliefs, you can change them.

There are an infinite number of core negative beliefs, and all of us have our own unique ones. But certain ones are so prevalent in our culture that most of us have them to some degree. Here are six of the most basic core negative beliefs that I have found (and each has many variations and outgrowths). I have included some possible clearing affirmations for each one.

1. *I am powerless.*
   I don't have the power to create my life. I'm a victim of outside circumstances. I'm helpless. Other people do things to me. I'm not responsible for what happens to me.
   Clearing affirmations: *I am a channel for the creative power of the universe. I am powerful. I am responsible for creating my life.*

2. *I have to sacrifice what I want due to scarcity.*
   There's not enough to go around of whatever I want. Therefore, I have to do without, or grab more than my share and cause others to do without. Here are some things that may feel scarce: money, love, time, energy, space, health, youth, vitality, employment, pleasure, and countless other things.

Clearing affirmations: *The universe is a source of plenty, and there is enough for all of us. My life is abundant. I have everything I truly need and desire.*

3. *Life is a struggle.*

    Things are hard. Life is difficult. It's not okay for my life to be easy, enjoyable, pleasurable, fun. If things are going well, watch out! Something bad is sure to happen. If I suffer enough in this life, I'll get my reward (hopefully) in the next.

    Clearing affirmations: *As I follow my inner guidance, life is a flow. Life is full and pleasurable. It's okay for me to relax and have fun.*

4. *I'm an unworthy person.*

    I don't deserve to be happy, healthy, wealthy. I don't deserve to be loved. Something's wrong with me. I'm not good enough. I'm not smart, talented, lovable (or whatever).

    Clearing affirmations: *I love myself. I accept myself. I deserve to be happy (healthy, wealthy, etc.). I deserve to be loved.*

5. *I fear failure, success, or power.*

    I'm afraid to take a risk, for fear I'll fail or succeed. If I fail, others will reject me. If I succeed, others will envy me or want something from me. I'll be isolated. I won't be able to uphold my image. I'll be too powerful. I'm afraid of my own power. If I own my power, I might misuse it.

Clearing affirmations: *It's okay for me to risk being myself. I don't need external validation. I validate myself. I trust my power. It's okay for me to try things and to fail. I learn from all my experiences. It's okay for me to be a success.*

6. *I don't trust myself.*

    I don't trust the universe. I'm afraid to trust my feelings, my intuition. I'm afraid there is no higher power to take care of me. I'm afraid to go with the power of the universe inside of me. I'm afraid to let go of my individual control and surrender to the higher force.

    Clearing affirmations: *I trust myself. I trust the higher power inside me.*

There are many other core negative beliefs as well, so be open to discovering your own. Deeply recognizing a core negative belief in yourself is 99% of the process of letting go of it. It will probably take a while to dissolve, but it will be on its way out, once you really see and feel how it has been operating in your life. You can help to dissolve it by using an affirmation. To find a good affirmation, first write down your negative belief as accurately as you can, in one sentence. Then write a positive statement that corrects and counteracts the negative one. For example:

Negative belief: *I'm afraid of my power because I'm afraid I'll hurt someone.*

Clearing affirmation: *I trust my power because it always causes me to act for the highest good.*

The following exercise will help you get in touch with your negative belief in any given situation.

The Core Belief Process

This process is best done with a partner, but you can also do it alone. If working with a partner, one of you asks the questions and the other answers them (take about two or three minutes for each question), all the way through to the end. Then switch roles and have the other person ask the questions, while the other partner answers.

If you do this process alone, you can write down your answers to each question, answer them silently to yourself, or speak into a tape recorder and listen back.

Sit silently for a moment, eyes closed, and get in touch with that part of yourself that is powerful and responsible — the creator of your experience. Now think of a particular situation, problem, or area of your life where you need to expand your awareness or become more conscious.

Now answer the following questions:

1. Describe the problem, situation, or area of your life that you want to work on. Take three or four minutes to talk about it generally.

2. What negative thoughts, fears, worries are you having? Take three or four minutes to describe these thoughts.

3. What physical sensations are you feeling?

4. What emotions are you feeling? (Describe the *emotion* — e.g., fear, sadness, anger, guilt. Do not describe the *thoughts* you are having about it.)

5. What is the worst thing that could happen in this situation (what is your greatest fear)? Suppose that happened. Then what would be the worst thing that could happen? What if that happened? Then what would be the *very worst thing* that could happen?

6. What's the best thing that could happen? Describe the ideal way you'd like it to be, your ideal scene for this area of your life.

7. What fear or negative belief is keeping you from creating what you want in this situation? Once you have explored this question, write your negative belief in one sentence, as precisely as you can. If you have more than one, write each of them down.

8. Create a clearing affirmation to counteract and correct the negative belief. Here are some guidelines:
   a. The affirmation should be short, as simple as possible, and meaningful for you.
   b. It should be in the present tense, as if it's already happening.
   c. It should use your name. Example: *I, Jeff, am a worthy person. I deserve to be loved!*
   d. The affirmation should *directly* relate to your core negative belief and turn it into a positive, expansive one. Some examples:
      Negative belief: *The world is a dangerous place. I have to struggle to survive.*
      Clearing affirmation: *I, Lucinda, now know how to take good care of myself and*

keep myself safe. The world is a safe place for me.

Negative belief: *Money corrupts people.*

Clearing affirmation: *The more money that flows into my life, the more power I have to do good for myself and others.*

Your affirmation should feel exactly right for you. It may cause a strong emotional feeling; if it's not right, try changing it until it is.

9. Reinforce your affirmation:

   a. Say your affirmation silently to yourself in meditation, picturing everything working out perfectly.

   b. If you have a partner, have your partner repeat your affirmation aloud to you, using your name and looking deeply into your eyes. After he/she says it, you say, "Yes, I know!" Repeat this process ten or twelve times. Then *you* say your affirmation and your partner says, "Yes, it's true!"

   c. Write your affirmation ten or twenty times a day. If negative thoughts arise, write them on the back of the page, then keep writing the affirmation on the front until you feel clear about it.

POSITIVE ENERGY LISTS

• • •

Positive energy lists can be used to help you tune into and appreciate yourself and your life. This process gets your positive energy flowing, and automatically helps you open up to your creativity.

Self-Esteem List

Make a list of the things you like about yourself, no matter how small or large — whatever you consider to be your positive qualities. Each of us has many positive qualities, and often we don't take time to acknowledge or appreciate ourselves. The better you feel about yourself and the more you appreciate yourself, the happier and more loving you will be, the more your creative energy will flow, and the greater contribution you can make to the world. Think of things you like about your body, your personality, your character, the ways you relate to people, your intellect, and your spiritual nature. Write down *everything,* even if you feel silly doing it. This is a very important exercise. Keep adding to this list all the time.

Success List

Make a list of everything you feel you are a success at, or have been a success at, or have done successfully at some time in your life — small things and big things. Include all areas of your life, not just work. Write down everything that has meaning for you, even if it might not to someone else. The purpose of this list is to acknowledge yourself and your abilities, which increases your energy for creating and accomplishing more. Keep adding to this list all the time with things that you have accomplished successfully each day.

Appreciation List

Make a list of everything you can think of that you are especially thankful for, or that you especially appreciate having in your life. Making and adding to this list can really open up your heart, and help make you aware of the many riches you've already created in your life that you may take for granted. This list increases your realization of prosperity and abundance on every level, and thus your ability to manifest.

Self-Appreciation List

Now list all the ways you can think of to be good to yourself, nice things that you can do for yourself, things that are just for your own pleasure and satisfaction. They can be small or large, but make some of them be things that you can do every day, and then do them! This increases your sense of well-being and satisfaction, which helps you to come from a clearer space in creating your life. Add to this list as you think of new things.

Outflow List

Make a list of all the ways that you can outflow your energy to the world and to others around you, both generally and specifically. Include ways that you outflow money, time, love and affection, appreciation, physical energy, friendship, touching, and your special talents and abilities. Follow through on actually doing these things as you feel like it. Add to this list when you think of new things.

Healing & Assistance List

Write down the names of any people you know who need healing or special support or assistance of any sort. Then write down an affirmation (a positive statement in the present tense) describing the desired reality you would like to help them create. Then every time you look through your notebook, you'll be giving them a positive "boost" of your energy. What they do with that energy is up to them. You can't influence or control them, but you can support them in what they feel is best for them.

More Creative Visualization Techniques & Practices

To help you get to the point where it's natural to think creatively and to use your imagination positively, there are many different techniques that you can practice. Following are three favorite creative visualization techniques, which you can learn easily and use regularly if you want to. The first one is a meditation process, the second is a writing process, and the third is an art process.

Pink Bubble Technique

Sit or lie down comfortably, close your eyes, and breathe deeply, slowly, and naturally. Gradually relax more and more deeply.

Imagine something that you would like to manifest. Imagine that it has already happened. Picture it as clearly as possible in your mind, or simply feel or sense it.

Now imagine that you can surround your fantasy with a pink bubble. Put your goal inside the bubble. Pink is the color associated with the heart, and if this color vibration surrounds whatever you visualize, it will bring to you only that which is in perfect affinity with your being.

Now let go of the bubble, and imagine it floating off into the universe, still containing your vision. This symbolizes that you are emotionally letting go of it, turning it over to the higher power of the universe to bring it to you.

You can do this process one time and let go of it completely, or you can do it regularly for a while. If you want to do it regularly, I recommend doing so every morning when you wake up, and again at night before going to sleep.

Ideal Scene Technique

Think of a goal that is important to you. It can be a long-range or short-range goal. Write down the goal as clearly as possible in one sentence.

Underneath that, write *Ideal Scene,* and proceed to describe the situation exactly as you would like it to be when your goal is fully realized. Describe your scene in the present tense, as if it already exists, in as much detail as you wish.

When you have finished, write at the bottom:

This or something better is now manifesting for me in totally satisfying and harmonious ways, for the highest good of all concerned.

Then add any other affirmations you wish, and sign your name.

Now sit quietly, take a few deep breaths, and visualize your ideal scene in a relaxed state of mind, and repeat your affirmations.

Keep your ideal scene in your journal, in your desk, near your bed, or hang it on your wall. Read it often, and make appropriate changes when necessary. Bring it to mind during your meditation periods.

Treasure Map Technique

Making a treasure map is a very powerful process, and one that is fun to do. A treasure map is an actual, physical picture of your desired reality. It is valuable because it forms an especially clear, sharp image, which can then attract and focus energy into your goal. It works along the same lines as a blueprint for a building.

You can make a treasure map by drawing or painting it, or by making a collage using pictures and words cut from magazines, books, cards, photographs, lettering, and so on. Don't worry if you are not artistically accomplished. Simple, childlike treasure maps are just as effective as great works of art! Basically the treasure map should show you in your ideal scene, with your goal fully realized.

Here are some guidelines to help you make the most effective treasure maps:

- You can create a treasure map for a single goal or area of your life. You might want to make one treasure map for your relationships, one for your job, one for your spiritual growth, and so on. If you prefer, you can create one treasure map with all the elements included.

- You can make a treasure map any size that's convenient for you. You may want to keep it in your journal, hang it on your wall, or carry it in your pocket or purse. I usually make mine on light cardboard, which holds up better than paper.

- Be sure to place yourself in the picture. For a very realistic effect, use a photograph of yourself. Otherwise, draw yourself in. Show yourself being, doing, or having your desired objective — traveling around the world, wearing your new clothes, being the proud author of your new book, opening up to your higher self, etc.

- Show the situation in its ideal, completed form, as if it already exists. You don't need to indicate how it's going to come about. This is the finished product.

- Use lots of color in your treasure map to increase its power and impact on your consciousness.

- Make it look believable to yourself.

- Include some symbol of the infinite that has meaning and power for you. This could be an "Om" sign, a cross, Christ, Buddha, a sun radiating light, or anything that represents universal intelligence or God. This is an acknowledgment and a reminder that everything comes from the infinite source.

- Include affirmations on your treasure map. For example: *Here I am driving my new hybrid gas and electric car.* Be sure to also include the cosmic affirmation: *This or something better now manifests for me in totally satisfying and harmonious ways, for the highest good of all concerned.*

The process of creating your treasure map is a powerful step toward manifesting your goal. Now just spend a few minutes each day quietly looking at it, and every once in a while throughout the day give it a thought. That is all that's necessary.

Practicing the Techniques

If you like, you can combine all these techniques to develop one particular goal. First, pick a goal. It can be on any level — material (e.g., a house, a car, a job, etc.), emotional, or spiritual. Choose something that is important to you, something fairly realistic and believable, and that you feel pretty positive about. Write your goal, simply starting with: "My goal is…"

State your goal as an affirmation by writing it as a sentence in the *present* tense, as if it were *already* true. (Make sure you don't use words like "I *will* have" or "I *want* to do" that place your goal in the *future,* not the present. Use phrases like "I *now* have," "I am *now* doing," and so on.) Keep your affirmation as short and simple as possible.

Close your eyes, take a few deep breaths, and relax your mind and body. Say your affirmation to yourself a few times, imagine that it is now true, and see how it feels to have your desire come true. Then imagine putting it into a pink bubble, tossing the bubble into the air, and letting go of it. Consciously affirm, "I am turning this over to the higher intelligence of the universe within me, to guide me in creating it." You can also repeat the cosmic affirmation, "This or something better is now manifesting for me in totally satisfying and harmonious ways, for the highest good of all concerned."

Try writing an ideal scene for this particular goal. Write a few paragraphs describing this goal in as much detail as possible as if it were already true (in the present tense). If you have any trouble doing this, see if you can mentally project yourself into the future, to the time when this goal has been fully realized. Then pretend you are writing a letter to your best friend, describing the situation in detail. For example, if your goal is to create a job you like, then you would write a description of your ideal job as if you were already there, describing where you work, what you are doing, your surroundings, your co-workers, how much you are getting paid, and so on.

After you have written your ideal scene, try drawing a treasure map. Remember to be relaxed and playful about your artistic ability, or lack of it. This is for fun! And it's also very effective.

You may find, as you go along, that your affirmation changes somewhat. Or perhaps you will realize that a different affirmation seems better, more accurate, or more important to you. Always be flexible and open to changes.

How to Proceed with Creative Visualization

Once you have completed each of the previous exercises, you can continue to work on creatively visualizing your goal, if you choose, by practicing the pink bubble technique, repeating your affirmation in meditation every morning and night, and writing affirmations (with the clearing process) every day or a couple of times a week for a while.

If you have other goals that you want to work on, you can go through the same process with each of them. When you are starting to learn creative visualization, it is usually a good idea to focus on only one or two things at a time for the sake of simplicity. Later, you may find that you can focus on more things at once, or you may want to continue to keep it simple.

Keep visualizing and playing with a particular goal as long as you have energy for it and it feels good to do so. If you start feeling bored with it, or discouraged, it may be time to let it go for a while. Often when you let something go and forget it for a while, you will later realize that it has manifested in your life while you weren't looking, so to speak!

There really are no rules about how to use creative visualization. Each person is different, and each situation is different. I can make suggestions based on my experience, but the ultimate authority for you is *you*. You must experiment to find out what feels good to you and what works effectively for you, and this will probably change from time to time. Trust your own intuition and do what feels right for you.

Sometimes people get frustrated and annoyed with themselves because they don't use the techniques regularly, even though they've found that they work. Don't use creative visualization as another reason to criticize yourself! Trust yourself. If you don't feel the energy to do this work regularly, there may be a reason that only your inner self knows about as yet.

If you feel like doing it and have a sense that you need to make a regular practice of this for a while, then do it. You will find it very rewarding. If you don't, don't worry about it. The most important thing is that you've got the understanding that you are responsible for creating your life. If you can remember, moment by moment as you live your life, to be more aware of your thoughts and beliefs, and how you are creating your reality, you will be accomplishing a lot. Then, when you feel especially motivated by a particular desire or problem, go ahead and use the appropriate creative visualization techniques to work on it.

I wish you enjoyment and sucess in your use of creative visualization and affirmation.

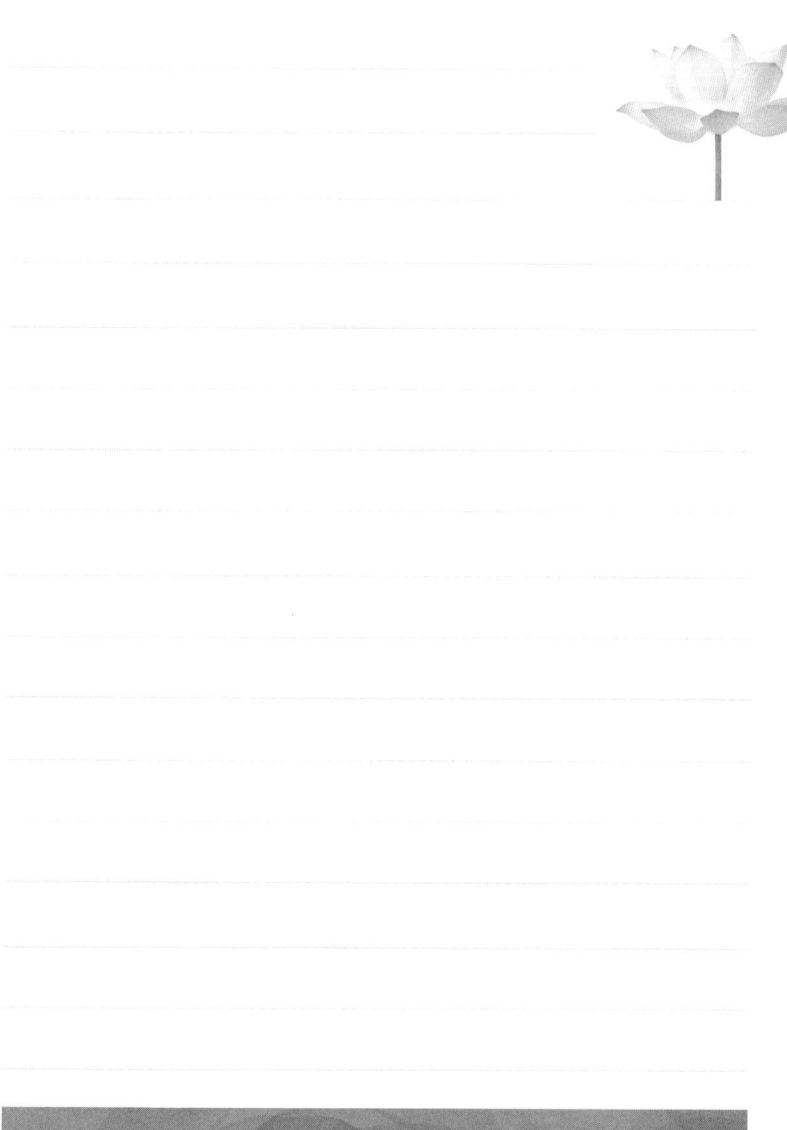

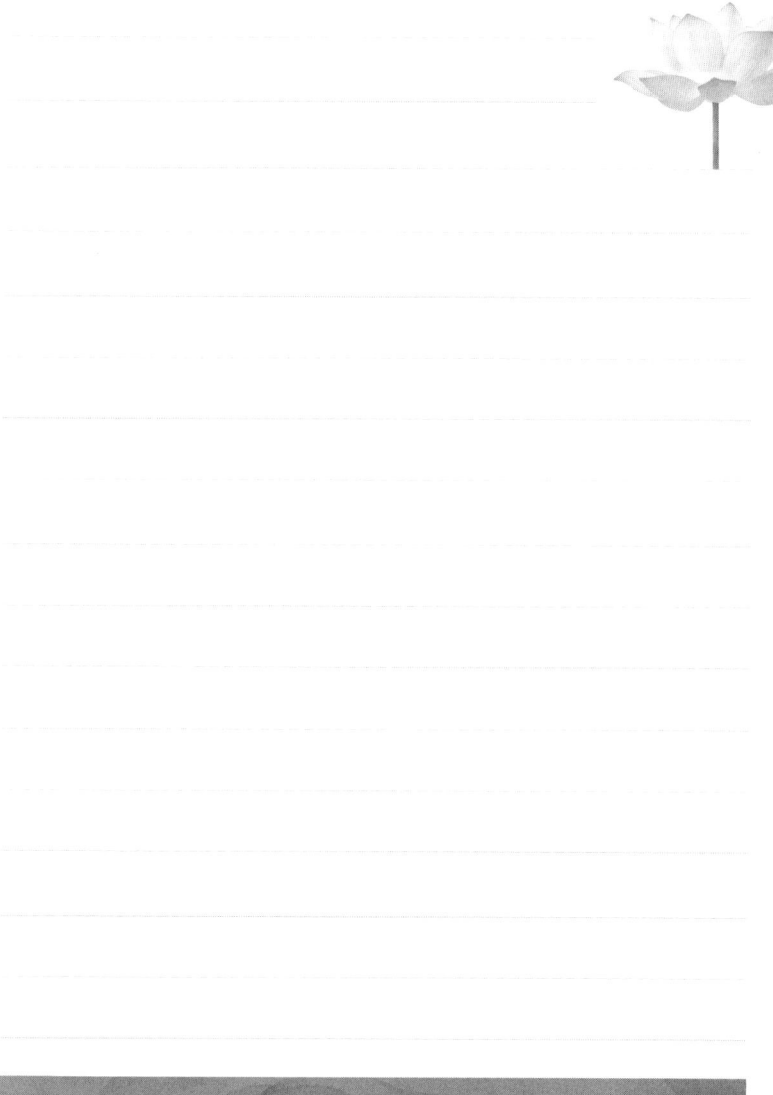

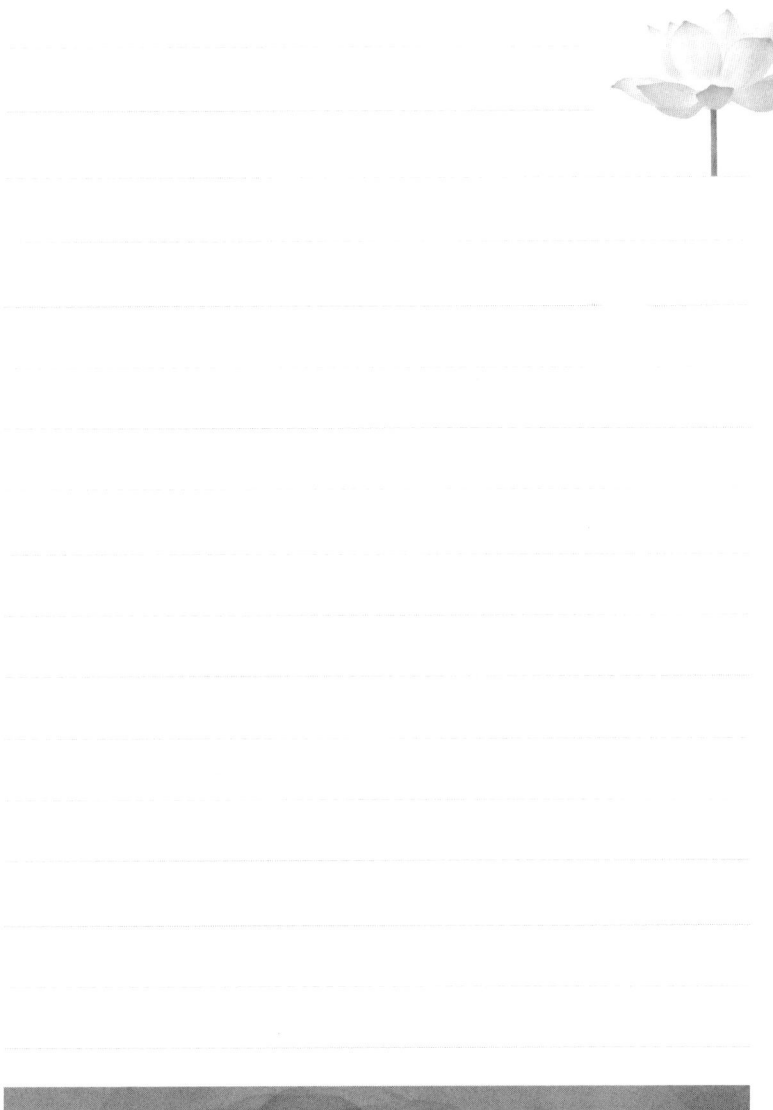

RECOMMENDED RESOURCES

Books and Audios

Creative Visualization: Use the Power of Your Imagination to Create What You Want in Your Life by Shakti Gawain. Nataraj Publishing/New World Library, revised edition, 2002. This classic guide is filled with meditations, exercises, and techniques that can help you increase your personal mastery of life.

The Creative Visualization Workbook by Shakti Gawain. Nataraj Publishing/New World Library, 1982. A large-format book, specially designed to accompany *Creative Visualization,* leads you step-by-step in planning your goals.

Creative Visualization audio set by Shakti Gawain. Nataraj Publishing/New World Library, 1995. The unabridged audio version, read by the author on two cassettes or two CDs.

Creative Visualization Meditations audio by Shakti Gawain. Nataraj Publishing/New World Library, 1995. Meditations guided by the author on cassette or CD.

Creating True Prosperity by Shakti Gawain. Nataraj Publishing/New World Library, 1997. This book presents a new definition of prosperity that places importance on fulfillment of the heart and soul rather than simply on monetary gain.

Developing Intuition by Shakti Gawain. Nataraj Publishing/New World Library, 2000. Clear, practical guidance and simple exercises that show us how to develop our intuitive ability.

The Four Levels of Healing by Shakti Gawain. Nataraj Publishing/New World Library, 1997. Identifying, balancing, and integrating all four levels of existence — spiritual, mental, emotional, and physical.

Living in the Light: A Guide to Personal and Planetary Transformation by Shakti Gawain (with Laurel King). Nataraj Publishing/New World Library, revised edition, 1998. This book offers practical advice for developing our intuitive inner guidance and learning to follow it on a daily basis.

Meditations audio set by Shakti Gawain. Nataraj Publishing/New World Library, 1989. Four powerful meditations: Contacting Your Inner Guide, The Male and Female Within, Discovering Your Inner Child, and Expressing Your Creative Being, guided by the author on two cassettes or two CDs.

The Path of Transformation: How Healing Ourselves Can Change the World by Shakti Gawain. Nataraj Publishing/New World Library, revised edition, 2000. This book gives us the tools for healing ourselves on all levels — spiritually, mentally, emotionally, and physically, and shows that as we heal ourselves, we transform the world.

Awakenings: A Daily Guide to Conscious Living by Shakti Gawain. Nataraj Publishing/New World Library, 1991. Daily meditations explore how to accept and balance the many aspects of ourselves, and how to live with the dualities and polarities of life. Each entry concludes with an inspiring affirmation.

Reflections in the Light: Daily Thoughts and Affirmations by Shakti Gawain. Nataraj Publishing/New World Library, revised edition, 2003. A book of daily insights and affirmations.

Return to the Garden: A Journey of Discovery by Shakti Gawain. Nataraj Publishing/New World Library, 1989. Shakti tells the story of her life and her journey of consciousness, and discusses the evolutionary process on earth.

Coming Home: The Return to True Self by Martia Nelson. Nataraj Publishing/New World Library, 1992. An inspired explanation of life on earth and what it's all about.

Embracing Our Selves by Dr. Hal Stone and Dr. Sidra Stone. Nataraj Publishing/New World Library, 1989.

This brilliant book shows us the many different "selves" within us and how we can integrate them to find balance and harmony.

Embracing Your Inner Critic by Dr. Hal Stone and Dr. Sidra Stone. HarperSanFrancisco, 1992. Gives practical help for effectively dealing with self-criticism.

Meet Your Inner Critic audio by Dr. Hal Stone and Dr. Sidra Stone. Delos, Inc., 1990. Further help for dealing with the inner critic.

The Nature of Personal Reality (A Seth Book) by Jane Roberts. New World Library/Amber-Allen Publishing, 1994. An excellent explanation of how we are each totally responsible for creating our own reality.

Workshops

Shakti Gawain conducts workshops throughout the United States and in many other countries. She also leads retreats and training programs in California and in Hawaii. For more information or to join her mailing list, contact:

Shakti Gawain
P.O. Box 377
Mill Valley, CA 94942
Phone: (415) 388-7140
E-mail: staff@shaktigawain.com
www.shaktigawain.com

ABOUT THE AUTHOR

Shakti Gawain is the bestselling author of *Creative Visualization, Living in the Light, Reflections in the Light, The Path of Transformation, Developing Intuition, Creating True Prosperity,* and several other books. A warm, supportive, and articulate facilitator, Shakti has been a pioneer in the field of personal growth for three decades and is internationally renowned for her inspirational workshops. She has taught thousands of people how to trust and act on their own inner truths, and how to release and develop creativity in every endeavor. Shakti and her husband, Jim Burns, live in Mill Valley, California, and Kauai, Hawaii.

Nataraj Publishing,
a division of New World Library,
is dedicated to publishing books and other media
that inspire and challenge us to improve
the quality of our lives and our world.

For a catalog of our fine books and audios, contact:

New World Library
14 Pamaron Way
Novato, CA 94949

Telephone: (415) 884-2100
Fax: (415) 884-2199
Toll-free: (800) 972-6657
Catalog requests: Ext. 50
Ordering: Ext. 52

E-mail: escort@nwlib.com
www.newworldlibrary.com